Are We Not Drawn . . .

Also by Peter Philpott

The Bishop Stortford Variations
What Was Shown
Some Action Upon The World
Textual Possessions

Are We Not Drawn . . .

PETER PHILPOTT

Shearsman Books
Exeter

Published in the United Kingdom in 2009 by
Shearsman Books Ltd
58 Velwell Road
Exeter EX4 4LD

www.shearsman.com

ISBN 978-1-84861-024-8
First Edition

Copyright © Peter Philpott, 2009.

The right of Peter Philpott to be identified as the author of this work
has been asserted by him in accordance with the
Copyrights, Designs and Patents Act of 1988.
All rights reserved.

Acknowledgements
Portions of this sequence have been published on/in
the following websites/magazines:
Ian Seed's *Shadow Train*, Adam Fieled's *P.F.S. Post*
& Andrew Nightingale's *Liminal Pleasures*.

Are We Not Drawn . . .

"Are we not drawn onward, we few, drawn onward to new era?"
*(Anne Michael, **Fugitive Pieces**)*

for Ginie

Book I

The Book of Dawns

A 1

are you listening to this
                        seriously
can what comes here
                 catch you
hide you
        ideas of youth echoing
like something out of the Ice Age
                      multiple segues sluicing down the piste
if you were listening
                your eyes, your fingertips
on the white open page
                there
can you hear
        me write
here this pen moves
                across the line
light
    moulded & channelled
like meaning
          across

2

we blow the fill
                and shatter
every morning
                without warning
all the tricks
              you like 'em best
just
    don't hold your breath here
we are fragile today
                fraxile & fractuous
we'll take anything that comes
                      usually like buses
trundle trundle
                they caught it on the wire
elegance of their points
                      cream paintwork & the borough arms
all along the promenade and back
                      oh the air fills your lungs
freshly blown
            shattered suburbs go
singing
      the one-way ride
morning light
            to imperfect nostalgia

3

   not
      not anything
   think in no
         way can this be
   happening or whatever
               the little line of words
   breaks
      doesn't matter, no
   how it is the voice does it
            reaches
   the end of that lie
        and back
   this time
      and this
   time
     this time
   this time
       not
   not really
       anything

4

drawn to dawn
                don't don
in big rounded letters
                        all that emptiness
that assonance & misery
                              spattered like a crime scene
CSI Somewhere
                cold, still, unpeopled
wherever you looked
                      you heard their voices
loudest I think
              there then
if focused on
              inescapable
also judgement
                  played out long
in a fair hand now
                  out loud
say it!
      fictive action

5

onward
        a noble name
onward
        redolent of meaning
onward
        and then another
pages ripped out
                this book was never complete
those gaps
        authored in an autistic sort of way
what they led to
        more
but always you see
                difficult
the other side of that tear or break
                          what comes again
another
        constantly onward

6

few images
        those here valueless
got at repeatedly
            gnawed at
better ignored
        I knew it
for you
      the words might break out
like a river in a city
            immediate
you can get out
        like the birds
wheeling over it
          mobile fluxions
and the light
        creeping in
and the self-evident complexity
                  internal dialectic
breaks up
      this place at once

7

new every morning
                    nude & mute
mourning
        the light's sullying & staining
until the end
          hidden glows play, mutate
slowly dying
        do you
see this
        the immensity of the one process
distilling
        the day's dew
newly done
          every day
different
        the same each morning

8

era that was
                not so much heroic
a long march
                few would survive
an embarrassment
                      the slow slide
the tipping point
                    reached unobtrusively
nothing heroic
                a still point
where the irrecoverable
                    becomes our bride
the veil lifted
            on the delusion we had bought
into
    the fracture, the tip
beyond this point
                only heroes go

B 9

it's the second go
>> we're not happy
that metaphor's melted
>> it's global irony
which clung
>> and you caused it!
these words
>> don't stay long
what were
>> you thinking of
as if you are
>> a kind of reverse Houdini
I will stay here
>> ting! ting!
it's gone
>> off without you now
that preposterous shape
>> a mess of scree
and you want to stay
>> here again
oh this isn't vertigo
>> cue not far to go
cut puns fast — oh
>> it bucks
and buckles up
>> a long way down now

10

shakily drawn up
                like peanuts about to be hanged
sing gibberish to authority
                        good educational values
1950s or 1490s?
            they burst the bus
those who are free
                dance in the air
those who know they aren't
                      sing harder
the wind blows
            also tonight
are you nostalgic
              or simply on the side of power?
get off
      and walk!

11

trying not to
        these phrases do just come
oh yes?
    like this
or sometimes that
        a rip
and the whole page
        gets bundled up & out
pick it up!
    you claim it
all your own original work
        some kind of value added
that page
    real benefit to human lifestyle
a strange illusion
    keeps moving onward

12

at one obscure time
                        Imagine it now
tinted
      stirred by the brightness of this evening
lurid
      desperately clear
as if the world's about to end
                        slip into the sea
we wouldn't want that
                  blinkety blink!
it's crept back
            the opposite of waking
control it while you can
                    that trick mechanism
out of the one little seed
                  shall grow a universe
where every bit touches another
                          taste emptiness, earthling!
cold, clear, lurid
            gorgeous golden browns
imagine waking up in the cinema
                      how beautiful & various this world
the one we don't live in
              imagine

13

    to see beyond
               foolish & dangerous
    where rivers go to
               come from
    equally uncertain
               mud mostly
    a foggy place
               too steep, flat
    few ideas just
               how to cope here
    how then do we know this is real?
                            it is so dirty
    and that's the good thing
                     to relax into imperfection
    let what's beyond
               sweep around
    curled
        & unconstrained

14

a taste of pus
                the smears of mucus
this too is to be human
                        they say
a good day
          nearly
I'm losing nostril hair
                      no one ever reported this
CSI just off the M11
                    found traces of basil
you didn't know
                this was all flooded, did you?
everything changed
                  its essence remained intact
nonexistence helps
              though the world
wears down
          it's Essex
at that familiar sign
              the road winds up
carrying the criminals & the commuters
                            their girlfriends & their wives
they, too, are human
              I am told
drawn to the scene
              as if it meant something

15

   it always comes out
                      minor explosions of pus
   what is this doing here?
                      encumbering comes the answer
   a certain level of difficulty
                      like shrinkwrapping around everything
   won't bloody budge
                      OK let's move onward here
   firstly that
          locate your last position
   then run
        you'll never leave
   what was promised
                horribly fulfilled
   in the long run
            we all lose our breath
   it goes on
       we won't
     it stops

16

you every morning
                you are remote
more in
      delight's alliances restrained
trill it then
        Eden grows, perambulates
slow leaf to ring
          to you
seize it
      the incentives follow this possesses
do you ring
        the dado
never leaden in
           ephedrine
diffract
      this Amish morning

17

they go
        all the same
no one made this hall of fame
                without some major shit
that
    or a good name
something that echoed
            OK
it's a kind of tic or loop
              you can pull
out
    go
out
    into what's outside this
and that's
        all the same too
that era when
            there was difference
not outside
        ever
can't consider
        alter
our lonely
        the hero

C 18

you chose
> the four corners of the world centred here

you chose money
> water drawn across the smooth stone

you chose gold & silver
> roads radiating from this centre

you chose dominion
> village life managed for all

you chose the pain of crucified Christ
> calendars for the day & for the night work also

you chose your own desire & guilt
> walls that withstand earthquakes

you chose your immediate pleasure
> carved rocks that mirror mountains

you chose that anyone must die
> public feasts & ritual drunkenness

you chose to loose all ties
> the shining path through the mountains

you chose to break what was not yours
> the scarlet woven banners

you chose
> to tangle up the cords of knowing

you chose
> desolation

you chose
> this world removed of all animals and ghosts

you chose
> to crouch in the cold empty air

19

strange illusions, say
                there is some other way?
I like Perdido Street best
                then Finido
it gets foggier by the day
                onward!
that rush of climatic change
                a mere challenge to our skills
little things do not bother us
                & the big ones, well
we aim to ride them on
                a single point
below where the wave breaks
                will take us far over your homes
the whole thing beneath
                ends up muddy cardboard
but it'll be ours
        so we don't care
where we're going
                just riding easy now

20

curled and unconstrained
                             a river or lane
laid across the grid
                         a new dimension
that other way out
                        can't guard it
recognition of the route
                        it's open
merely can't be thought of
                         what the heck?
few believe this
                  not so much here
peer-assessed science
                        optimism of the will
at the worst
              there will still be an ocean
something other
                  to dive into
phew!
       they were close
but we
      are closer

21

    and what was
                gone
    my temper today
                the Greenland Ice Cap
    then all genetic diversity
                we are the choke-point
    where creation stutters
                begs for a Heimlich manoeuvre
    no one will administer
                the era
    let's be literal here
                is a problem
    the nature of this point
                so unstable
    we're fools to live here
                but
    well
        we just do now
    nothing more to gain
                from it
    here
        we are

22

this world's
        one of the best
I think
     when the evening hangs heavy
a bright golden light
                angelhair & urine
stains, yes?
       taints & tints
as if it really was
         "the best"
you know
      like the one upstairs
oh that one's
      just probably our favourite
and not
    briefly
for this light
      under the world
makes us see
     how
briefly
   we live

23

    the game sings
                really
    second time tonight
                  big writing
    cos we are tired now
                    the words floppier
    slightly more hysteric maybe
                      they say
    you're losing it
               but you just don't care
    this whole lot
               can vanish in the air
    or where
          we are
    the other side
              of the motorway box
    looking at
            this is sudden

24

once reached
                you're no longer there
oh silly boy, it's here!
                that point
is this
     always crumbling away
perpetual fall
              it's getting worse
yesterday I twitched
                that is a sorry mess
hold on
     please hold on

25

    I like the dapples most
                      graded flashbacks
    or the torch shots
                over here, Boyd
    our boys do it better
                    so fucking complicated
    I can't see where the bullet went
                          just vanished
    life's also like that
               a kind of motorway
    spattered with flowers & glass
                          everyone comes back
    they just stand around, you know
                          that's all
    mere presence of photons
                    draws onward
    desperate
        disparate already
    attracted also
            to the seen

26

bloody like the rest of us
                    OK?
is this position clear?
                        like white leaves
like plangent similes
                        like white smiles
we want to eat you
                    failing that
tear up the page
                move on
is it always quick here?
                    brisk
bloody brisk I'd say
              OK?

D 27

a filthy little Andaman Islander
                                        typical projection
I am all alone here
                don't ask
nature alas is dead
                the concrete in the clay
something in the old coffeeshop
                            just a bunch of chavs
one of them butted Ash
                      I reached for some weapon
culture, wide knowledge & savoir vivre
                              pretty fucking useless, hwah?
things have progressed
                  entropy somehow swept up on us
like a really good nervous breakdown
                              I don't go out much now
excuse my writing
                this line doesn't hold

28

inside the curtains
                         the room was real
nothing else
                 it all melted
paths through time
                        at the end a fine dust
heavy with poison
                      bring on the microbots!
endless cycles
               but they're slowing
you silly, I can't stay still
                        every line just different
who have you killed?
                         on whose deaths is our prosperity founded?
monuments
              and monuments
drawn backwards
                 we go onward
the angel
          a puppet of fire
the shining paths
                are redrawn

29

    golden boys
               drive buses here
must
    come
like the light
        straight through
the sun set
        behind the post-office
its light fills this room
              like wax the auditory meatus
neat, hunh?
        this world's pretty nifty tonight
launched
        on its old one way journey
we're getting near the pier
              get ready to descend
on the beach
        we all watch the sunset
all
   we ever do

30

how close?
                to what end and show?
close to these questions
                OK
still black water
                a drizzle
rubbish in the mud
                few ways out from here
baby
      we know the ways that don't work
think of your parents as an analogue computer
                                    testing how not to do it
we aren't that different
                    the algorithm backs up
stuttering like a crack
                a flaw in the disk of being
which way
        and to where?

31

    but not lost
             yet
    there in the hedgerow!
                straight over!
  I stand for liberty & land
                tell me where I am
  not lost yet
        my liberty, my land
  I keep
      terriers and a gaggle of old cars
  my nettle plantations
                at least the soil is black
  fatty
      can't have too much blood
  not losing this space
                my locus
  interlocution
          not elocution
  what I say
        is the sum of the seen

32

always questions?
                      my lawyers advise silence
a letter will follow
                      a whole sequence
this is another genre entirely
                      how fingers swell & shrink
strange, bony & wrinkled
                      all bloody inside still
at least that's in there
                      I don't question
your rights here
                      I question right itself
as you get older
                      you'll know what I mean
the whole structure
                      withers
blow it over
                      pass on
your fingers
                      tell who you are
no need
                      for questions yet

33

    I knew
            it would be all right
    at the end
               it must be, eh?
    where we've come to
                     is here
    in a single place
               we are all here
    everything's ended up
                    I can't believe it
    the arrangement
               really here
    it only lasts
         for a beat
    has happened
               everything has happened
    like it
        never
    spat out
        just here

34

so you're angry at yourself
                            again, Peter?
each time
        tripped over into a warm rage
open it
        on the verso — this
this point
        this stutter
this fall
        this break
closes everything up at once
                            yet opens new eras
not one
       many
era of bacterial domination
                            hiding in the rock
slow minds
        it isn't angry
waits
    until your anger dies

35

    hold on
           I didn't do this
    honestly I felt I managed something
                         but well, he'll bite
    it's these sudden dissolutions
                         like a brisk cold shower
    another light on the crime scene
                         the sun, the great sun, rising
    cars go by
           I'm left behind
    it wasn't my fault
           I didn't choose anything
    it was dawn
           the day just came
    all the rest
           happened

E 36

all that
        oh the grand gesture
scattering shit
                good for gardenias
where did you get it from
                        what obscure bodily process?
where the metabolism reached tipping point
                                self-referential singularity
jargon
       for the birds, man, just
leave it there
              & gesture emptily
hands flapping
              leave the coffee shop now
I think you did it
              and if you didn't
we can convince you
                you did
you do it
       you do it

37

hey, they've just stolen the election!
                                          no
it was drawn
        power always wins
you poor schmucks
                do you think this place yours?
gallivantin' through it since we landed
                              way back
good manoeuvrin', yeah
                    but the game plan is ours
all empires are
        sorry — brute fact
just ways of burying the dead change
                              a few names
lonely though
        sitting still
in
   the high cold

38

at dawn
        a red glow like plums
oh Victor how you are changed!
                      the contrails begin to glint
will we survive our own destruction?
                        some question, hunh?
it'll all come back
            and it won't be pleasant
oh no it'll be
            Onward Christian Soldiers — no thanks!
do you really think that end you aim at
                      is one you'll benefit from?
only Mr Capital
            and he's not real
the dawn's glow
            the summit's light
monuments of surpassing beauty
                      who built them?
who asked that question?
                step forward

39

on the tramway to the sunset
                          sweet like a mouth
the sea was grey, Johnny
                 where you came from
and the rain cold
            on the burning cities
or was it refraction?
                 what is at the horizon?
I don't want to reach it
                 this world's promise fulfilled
don't let it do that!
            turn up the sound now
close the curtains
             even if they're drawn
shut out
       shut it out
get off the bus
            the sea is grey enough

40

I can't read this
    only dyslexics are that creative
this fascination with words
     won't work
it can't help you here
     in this muddy place
few signposts
   fewer maps
where the river goes
     as obscure as where it comes from
you think
  ah, metaphor or symbol
it's not that easy
   more like blindness
like the loss of all sense of direction
      adimensionality
like something horrible & obvious
     you can't name it
it
 names you

41

every time
        anger
comes again
        grows at the throat
what have we done
            now?
I can't say
        haven't managed it well
we are at this world's exact centre
                its dumb end
what we have done
        we have done to ourselves

42

everything already thought of
                                sort of goes
ready made language blocs obtrude
                                      Sloughlike
the cold hits the bowels
                        now!
we have come a long way
                        M11, M25, M
all of it at night
                    you don't know these lights
I can't help it that my fear of losing out here
                                      loss of control, of sense
the language is another
                    I'm another
the consciousness of all these cars
                                arriving here just
open the box
            oh jewels of the scene

43

who am I listening to?
                        who
am I listening
          to?
who
    connects across
then loses it all
              an empty proposition
who am I listening?
                    to whom
to who
       you can tell it's night
just don't answer the questions
                              whose questions?
who's question?
                who is
the question
          bloody hell I want
to stop
      I want
who
    who
who
    wants
to
   who

44

I'm swamped
              and pinched
I know what I ought to do
                      and don't
dream of escape
              a ship
a different shape
                a landscape
a salt charm
              the split flint
the hardness
              the encumbrance
to be aware
              the grin of this world
fight against
              sufficient to know
there is your hand
                  the jar, the new
the force of this
              never here

45

made me angry
        each moment
forged anew
        did you think for consistency?
among the brute materials
        how it's pushed & harmed
do you really think you could control that?
        oh boy, that's another era
gone
    wandered away from this town
everyone leaves you
        & their cloying love
is what actually nourishes
        & the occasional rage
I name this feeling
        my fingernail is about to fall out
am I made less
        how much will I lose?
at the end
    everything

46

whose word matters here?
        it is a fractured discourse
OK
  we've got that
& next?
    the angle of entry
traces of blood
      any residual DNA
don't knock anything!
       letters grow in spontaneously
it was a crime against spelling
         consummation fucking itself
oh draw the veil
     close the car door
drive out
   you can't get back
to a point before this
      they're all going
to come here
    any way

47

of which
       the rules say
it won't last long
            even its pretence more effective
I react to signifiers not things
                 I like the taste better
remember the seaside tram?
                the curve of the esplanade?
beyond it
      nada
it could end here
          with one simple word
but it'll drag out its wounded bulk
                    hide in the shrubbery & suffer
if sounds could be illegible
            like maybe the night is
I'm not happy
        but no word is these days
we're getting closer
           like rain

Book II:
Of Live Intent

F 48

what we do?
          what?
let's interrogate
            I think your ideology critique is good
just a little negative
              can it reach every last spot
of that old shit still in the teeth
                  well
faking various voices doesn't help
                    nor hinder
whose have we reached?
              can we leave?
can we pay the bill please
                & not with everything we've got
let's please just take something
                run
onward & inward
            I'd be in on that
that
   and the taste still of good coffee
fresh in the mouth
            bitter & rich

49

at dawn
  what is drawn
appears just like that!
     faint indentations darken
the whole field glows
    illimitably illumined
every time
  every time it happens
something bad
   maybe they too will pass
in the cold air they will vanish
      you must make a family
don't include capital!
    don't include holy men!
only good men
   the pen runs out
include
  good men & women quick!
their children, their
    dawn

50

under this light
        no premeditation
satori straight
        like some old monk punches me
oh, crazy with enlightenment
                like a moth
like a match
        like all the signs in Soho
I am but a country boy
                what is it lures me so onward?
the shining path
        the dawn one time
the coloured lit emptiness
                at dawn one time
the world gone mysteriously soft
                often
this happens again
        comedic
I'd watch the lack of light
              on on on

51

it names who?
                      and where's the mud?
all I could see was white
                            a fine complex filiation
the present decay of writing
                                how do we get out?
who is writing this plot
                        a man of few words
a place of few paths
                    it was midnight
he walked along the riverbank
                              tried not to rhyme
I can't help myself
                    someone made me do this

advance then
            is slow

52

no
    we haven't managed at all well
worse
       every bit of it is fucked
rapaciously so
           I didn't say I loved him
at least I never did that
             what I was offered
you will be able to reconstruct
                 here where the road swings across
touches some power
          just
might have been different
            oh no, we're in Essex now
it's dawn
    so forth
they'll come and find out
           almost worse
than when we dragged the knives across our throats
                       shame
how we fucked up
       everything

53

I could draw up a list
     precise enough for you?
the mountains & the seas
      who has been killed
the routes of tramways
      all those drawn faces
suddenly on video phones
      height of our creation
how many have died
     opening up the spectra
the shining path
    no, you silly, it's invisible
but slowly fries the brain
      the eyes must cloud
list all the damage
    what will go on
what
  is lost

54

Happy New Year!
                the box of the seas opened
there was no adequate response
                       cannot be
we are losing
         we betrayed ourselves
all those night journeys
                     capital will cut its own throat
who can survive?
           in the interior
in the deep
       there might be
is there a dark place
           is there night?
always the lights of the convoys
                        like jewels, like tracer
traces and tears
           the light diffracts
once it's left us
            it won't come back

55

in an instance
            the owl might leave
a bloody mess behind
                  or do they swallow it whole?
like a hole
       who'll know?
I don't
    the reply is quiet
almost unheard
         but just distinct enough:
chink!
    clickety-click
onward and upward
              like a pair of 30s writers
chained to the dialectic
                & a savage realism
ravaged by owls
          haunted by fears
not escaping
       not listening
not hearing
     it right

56

some strings run out
                    I hear the static
sounds of the stars
                    an impossible presence
don't we crave?
                    an impossible physics
I knew
      yes I knew all of this
cut across the grid
                  just here!
athwart
        a new declension
I invent the illusory case
                      that the word acts
rather it trails
              unravels & feeds back
dusty & spongy
              like a ghost
please
      there are moments
pretty brief
          pretty brief at best

57

ch'era
        era
lippetty loopetty
                look!
that man gibbers in Italian too
                            well . . . uhh
only a little
            when my gumboils let me
and at that point
                yes, it is different
losing it, stranger
              here at the heart
the admission is admired
                      it is breathless
the mission is mired
                it's less by a fingernail
but not the same
            not even twice
I can't help reading it differently
                          no — but it doesn't matter anyhow
it's a ratchet, see
        no
going back
        only down

58

still crazy
        sometimes jaunting
action stops thought
                that's why life today is so busy
the roads all lead down
                    precipitously now
dawn happened a long time ago
                      it's an old old world
that ain't what it was
                and won't be nuthin'
funny voices can't disguise
                  exponential rates of destruction
will it loop around at some point
                      or fly
up or drown
        into the cold silence
rock
    or sky?

59

how
    did we get here?
and how
      do we get out
when
    there isn't any out?
umm, I
      think I'll need to phone a friend
not in these rules
          any answer and you lose
there is a good view
          nothing to get in the way
if it wasn't
      for the 'ouses in between
there aren't any
        and I don't like it
it doesn't like me
        I

60

I'm surprised
          half pissed
I know Nottingham too
                 achoo!
dream of escape
          every morning
when the light enters fresh
                flushed just liquid
I don't know
          I don't know
I never do
          dizzinesses rotate around us and
the air fills up our head
              some low hum
what's new?
         oh dear, nothing better
not onward
         but inward
at what level will it stop?
                I

61

a decent interchange came later
                                      out! out!
the plums were spurned
                          you royal bastards!
pick up the ripped pages
                          come off it then!
rosy-fingered Dawn in her negligée
                                    hot potatoes!
a page by China Miéville
                        bloody blungers!
and a moment of self doubt
                              the workers united!
there are many paths
                     who do you think you are!
fading like contrails
                        mardy-arsed little git!
onward with The Endeavour
                            onward! onward!
one word to bind them
                     don't go there!
the plumtree's branch shakes out its blossom
                                              shut up and look!

62

in place of mountains
                    just rain
I don't see it
        not at heart what there is
just drawn to it
            several similes
this awareness hurts
                  you get used to it
this world of epiphenomena
                        it doesn't give a shit
language — so funny sometimes
                      like a capricious & incompetent bureaucracy
we call this Grammar
                and then semiosis
also just plain word order
                        remember the trolley-buses?
remember the Inca funerals?
                        remember the flights at dawn?
drawn to it
      really

G 63

better not rich
               that is the problem
all that stuff
          people died to make it
don't you realise?
                   don't you know the cost of anything?
increasing prosperity
                   mortgages drawn upon our future
dead hands
          they'll pay — oh god — they'll pay
for what makes us easy
               fat with their loss
we have reached
            that point at which
there isn't any closure
               no stolen coffee
at the end
          of this dinner

64

OK, there was dawn
                         a mountain landscape
scenes of disaster
                what then?
what's the next thing?
                    isn't there one?
a sudden vast scattering
                      maybe without us
does talking centre this world upon us?
                                 oh shut up out there!
be still
      what you are
is that what you do?
               or can you
be separate?
         no
we're humans
            we meet
then we
      die

65

drawn down
        like a list of complaints
why don't you just celebrate?
                oh you silly brat
over-cerebral
        who'd salt your tail?
we may be
        all fucked up but
this world's full of it, eh?
                I don't think you need to develop it further
we've managed this present catastrophe
                        skipped all the others
chances are probably few & thin
                but, well, though the mode is tragic
this plot is open-ended
        go break the lines
speak something new
        now

66

new every morning
                the same place
calendars for the sky
                  & for the night work
the constant convoy of lorries
                        carrying in the slaves to toil
& each day before I get up
                  fear & sickness at the core
somatic tension
          what comes back?
not the light
            fresh each nacreous dawn
sunk into cloud at night
                a new calendar
toil in the dark
            so what comes back?
it is like the sea
            it is like the mountain

67

I can't help
          reading it differently
even with this earache
                  here I occur
era of high octane wordplay
                      plays out
you forgot the ratchet
                watch it!
and its muddy little harbour
                    no tramways here
(except — query?
            down from the Brendons with the iron ore
an unlikely industrial scenario
                    what we think is so
never permanent
            we live inside this process

H 68

I've drawn the short straw here
because at this point I'll stop
breaking up the lines to hold them still
like cats about to pounce or
the sea drawn back, audibly
to expose the simple fact we have reached
just this point here:
                       unique
untroubled by all the other stuff, I
know it inherits so much, but
it will try to push on fresh
like the perfect winter day it is, like
anything complete and of itself (which
everything is as much as part of it all
for though you can't read it twice
it will be more or less the same, a
fuzzy logic not Platonic ideal at
the point of its differentiation: a game
of stupid paradox, that contradicts itself
and is therefore true, beautiful, and full
                                    of live intent
& we ought to resist
                     that consonantal chaff
our language & our self
                          strimmed out and stalled

69

negotiations stall
                like oxen or cars
horses, tall horses
                in the midst of a hay of latinity
haze that could be
                even daze
try and hear this
                listen to what the shapes have drawn
bare hedges in the low sun
                listen to their shape this spring
a prayer
      a praise
a price
    surprise!
could we negotiate our way out
                or will a few problem clauses remain
viz they control capital
                and are controlled by it
and we ought to resist
                shattering

70

    who can remember it?
                       write it down then
    the diagram drawn on the whiteboard
                               it will be this
    the convoys go there
                       already losing the lines
    after that many repetitions
                         faint & worn down
    what has been worn
             up?
    a clear & ludicrous joke
                     lippetty loppetty usw
    that sense of humour is never forgotten
                             sometimes
    I think of killing myself
                     sometimes I do it
    I don't remember
                and do it again
    there are bright lights in the night
                           the sight
    fails
        maybe goes down

71

shut up and look!
                  no blossom in winter
cold & dryness
            like the high parching air
all sounds are strange
                  you didn't?
it is a landscape inimical to us
                      a bloody and a horrible place
it's where we are
              we have brought ourselves here
toiling in the mines
                we slave others
we enslave ourselves most
                  (see Hegel)
how can we rebel
              against our own decrees & systems?
bring it down!
            oh bring it
crashing down the trail
              back into Essex
back into anywhere
              where people still live
fragile
    as blossom

72

    it can't help it
               not at all it can't
d'y'ken?
        or coin?
can-can
        how much?
the stuttering
              expressive repetition
little explosions leave us
                  everything different
it was the era
        of eternal error
always was, duckie
              always was
the was wins
          we can't it
can't
    not
at all
    it can't

73

how could you have forgotten
                    oh your head is just full of porn
of old songs and the names of wines
                    you're just a Malkovich character
someone who grows gardenias
                    and whose body
opens like a pig
            there was a muddy river too
various tipping points
                    also doubts & redoubling
looking back
            I am my own reflection
and so on
        poses
posies
        the flowers give headaches
I am going out
            now

74

hum into this head then
      such a gesture!
bold as bunch of
    not that easy, son
the muddy river?
     isn't the right one
I just want to get back here
       not in this lifetime you won't
unless I work it sideways
     where is the outside?
here
  it's the lippetty lid, kid
spill it!
   like a bunch of fucking gardenias
no like something pure and totally itself
       on the shelf, elf
I can win the game
    how?
now?
  then

75

    the light
            oh the glint
    spicules in the dirt
                    its blackness is heavy
    ragged as trees
                under the clouds
    the world opens up
                 yellow light
    unstained and glowing
                    I'd go there
    onward
        from this point
    everything also comes
                   focused precisely
    on a single mica grain
                   a rotted leaf
    water trembling in a puddle
                      spilt on the floor
    the teeth of the dead dog
                    by god they are beautiful

76

what was was
              was
lightly soaked
              look!
it's hard as algebra
                      well, the non-linear kind
at least
        when I'm losing my gumboils
act at that point
                yes it is different
the admission is admired
                      it is breathless
the mission is mired
                less by a fingernail
but not the same
              not even twice
you can't help reading it differently
                                not knowing how it matters
how it all ratchets
              out of how it was
no going back
            onward!

77

it won't come back
                there are only 2 dimensions
pretty bloody complicated though
                        I mean you can't explain it
you can't explain 'it'
          or even
'explain'

it sublimed

there are traces
        here
and then a sort of build up
                you know it all by now
convoys, calendars, catastrophes
                      the motorway lights
with nacreous or fulvid dawns
              but
if something got lost
            who knows
what might not
          be new found

78

    the era of repetitions
                      begins again
    after the one of spring
                      perhaps dawn
    will come gain
                  probably ruined
    can you say
                  the same word twice?
    it isn't the same
                  it whirled
    what?
        wasn't the same
    was that?
            in a trice
    oh the cockatrice
                  is a merry bird
    but not one
            of this era
    I shall write it out
                said God
    and not repeat
             this error

79

it could end here
                with one simple word
'nothing' or 'friend' or 'gardenia'
                        nada
it's what they say to each other
                          how they gesture and smirk
how they stand against each other
                        drift & roll together
giant thundering grinding clouds
                        or whizz apart
did you see?
        all that space?
nothing is that beautiful
                that marks a friend of what is there
I won't say the other words
                    I shall be silent
but they'll say themselves
                squalid beasts
they stood and watched
              in awed silence
these are special days
              coming so near the end

80

who
    were you playing with just now?
who
    would want to play with you?
who
    do you think you are as good as?
gold maybe
        gardens
oh I blush
        this is easy manoeuvring
fish in a barrel, boy
        gardenias at The Grange
slippetty slip!
        you don't win
it's how
    the lines break
that's
    all
impersonality
        eats everything up

81

you call this special?
                      common or something
the nights anyway are a different calendar
                                we have to work them
in the day
        we try and reach the end of the tramlines
there! on The Esplanade!
                    I am making my own dreams
what happens with my eyes open
                          a fool recognises as reality
everyone is mad
            I am going to leave this town
walk out along the river
                    I don't mind the mud and drizzle
it'll take days
        several timeshifts possibly
can't be helped
            I'm not going back
what I have left
        won't be there

82

    get off and get out
                      that's all done then
    every last bit of plum blossom gone
                            and dawn now so onward
    we never see anything of her anymore
                            than a little trace of yellow silk
    colour & beauty
                  it isn't sentimental
    I'm reading Lee Harwood
                      (as you can probably guess
    that openness & un
                  sentimental acceptance of sentiment
    as part of what colours & composes
                          this world
    where the rain does fall musically
                            and a quiet TV hum can confirm
    human presence still
                  a passenger or friend
    someone to break bread with
                      you know
    it can be that simple
                sometimes

83

it's
    a long time between poems now
what was once
            23 times in 3 days
oh well
      how youth flies
it is a more long drawn out process
                    like negotiating the way
back across your troubles
            whish! whish!
the trains are toy trains
              but you are very little too
it is possible
      but very difficult
still no resolution
          only fresh influences
like sudden winter showers
              oh god like anything you fucking like
you can't predict
        that's certain

84

look
    the real guys are all sitting it out
height of chic is
        not to be here
everyone
      now conscious of your absence
like where the gumboils
          used to be
or the empty roads
       after the convoys
no more but difference then
          your fingernails are your own I think
I can't use them
     or follow these old traces
all faded into the dawn
         I'm losing touch with that whole scene now
the brickwork skimped here
        nothing under the soffits now
let's go please
     to another place and time
any such metaphor
      you know
onward
   yes
springing around
       these various attractions now

85

the worst journey is the world
                                    a huge dark stain
sorry, today's Tuesday
                        a warehouse not in Harlow
what exactly is your problem?
                                  I can't seem to fit it all together
dawn can be so fulvid
                   and little blue black clouds suddenly
do you think
          they bother to connect or make sense?
would you seriously complain
                          that each one just
coming & going
            new every et cetera
why do you want this thing to connect?
                                  let it rest
let it rest
        quietly now

86

    and any error was
                      not to use the word "love"
    a good word & strong
                      but will it bear repetition?
    like rain does
                the clicketty click of wheels
    like we've got in the same carriage
                            it'll take us to a certain date
    and then
          a new era of nothingness or loneliness
    ending at that little muddy harbour
                          I could turn
    spin
      like in a caesura'd line
    suddenly going up
                two halves
    I don't know
          if you or I'd be there
    I could
      still love you

K 87

let's eat impersonality
                        then
I tell you the word is love
                                also just strain & madness
bright & florid
                  as a bunch of
suddenly red, orange
                          a deep and total azure
this variety is unique
                      it's not double
better than the gardenias?
                            maybe so
certainly less predictable
                        except for its absolute intensity
eating up impersonality
                      like leaves do every colour
except green
            luminous virid shade
the indwelling presence of a god
                            another future will open
let's sit gently on the beach
                        watching the last sunset
these bright blossoming clouds
                            together

88

and what doesn't exist?
                        oh blimey, where . . . ?
tricks of punctuation really
                              it's what
and this is hard
                    because it is so direct and simple
is under all the days
                          & within each one
and all that isn't here
                          like a breath
a giant first grasp of air
                              or maybe something else
an etheric
            virtual flux of energy
drawn in
        and out of existence

89

can't fill in the spaces for you
                              not with what was meant
no one ever knows that
                          not with just any words either
but with what comes there
                        it doesn't

       it's more like a kingfisher

       flying & alighting

       the moment is stronger

       there might be
                    no way back
      ratcheted up
            one whole dimension
      the complexity of the array
                       affecting its properties
     what things are
              emergent from the vortices
     a whole new physics
            like light suddenly
the dark
      remains
            unfound

90

don't repeat
        that word
it may not be appropriate
                around here things are difficult just now
the little harbour's closed
                no one speaks Italian
the ratchet got stuck
                rusted as an industrial relic
I'm stuttering with cold
                the written language doesn't show this
what I'm really writing
                illegible
what the words say
            an indecipherable melange of cliche & catchphrase
the best
        maybe
this era can manage
                omission, admiration
\<insert the sound of a tape rewind\>
                        \<wind on the player\>
gloop! gloop!
            the error message comes twice

L 91

now
    the colours
their names
        imprecise & monochrome
pure & absolute
        subjective
glorious
    shared
and loved
        oh forget the muddy harbour & the river
the roads at night
        even the bright moving lights
which are hallucinations
        here & now
the colours of this place, the colours
        glow & immediate
supercharged & overladen
        glow like gardenias
like irises
    like primrose
like bright leaves
        like a bundle of rays
like the sun
    on wet pavements
the broken glass
    brick talus
every bit of muck
    glows

92

    a tired clarity
               this is getting near the end
    the days
         no stranger than we should have thought
    but didn't
         couldn't
see
  it is simple
what you dream
            came from somewhere
but I don't know
            where it goes
at what point
        it presses
against
     this dark cold face

93

it doesn't last longer than snow
        you must realise this
& not be drawn into any sentimental attachments
       hints of the old dawn, you know?
this is a clean operation
      financed by entropy
it'll all go
   value will sublime in white chubby clouds
as clumsy as these lines
      whatever systems of meaning you hold onto
switched off in the night
      abandoned like old tramways
great bulks of stone & timber
      we are all artists
we are the revolution too
     and what we struggle against
we are
  except this please
as always unsuspected as that brief transformation into white
           and laughter

94

but guys
   I wanted to say
someone wanted
     at the back of my throat
someone spoke
     it's not you or the world
it's what the poem is
     I don't want to forget love
I don't want to be losing I
     I'm sorry
maybe it won't be the poem
     that
moves onward
   piling up the words
I just want to choose from
     vast influx
fitter & rich
   admired & admitted
already
   unlost

95

unfound
        but not unfoundered
unfolded
        and infilled
unforgotten
              as rooms of dead cowboys
you can't go back
            only lie
I face backwards into this future
                      noting nothing
no tears neither
        at this point
where it plays put
           in this cold space
subliming
        like lines of verse
vanishing back
           within the vacuum
I can't hope
        I expect
and though love ends
            it won't
                will it?

96

    don't repeat
               not to us the word "love"
    after that one of spring
               or coin?
    an era of high octane wordplay
                     well . . . uhh
    it looks like we are
               stuck
    the poem's slow descent
                  quite decent really
    doesn't it
           remind you of how
    most things wind down
                 just gradually
    step by step
           slopetty slope
    the sense
        seizes
    up
     that is the direction
    and that
          remains
    read it differently
               or be
    you can't
          thank god
    but
      I could still love you

97

and I step forward
                now
poised
        in luminescence
essence
        sense
sins
    staining the great sky
like a sexual flush
                oh, it's easy
and also
        so difficult to do
to carry through
                from dawn
I don't care
        I don't care
what I have done
                I
am here
        onward

98

somehow
        same how?
smile
    I love you
in the darkness
        and the dawn
ignore revisionism
          I salute the myth
by this I'll die
      probably
it is a long way from
          where I started
long ways
    from where I thought I would end up
there is still a little time
         or is it distance?
or the mountain
       (which will not move
the hillside
    where the convoys led to
the tramways
    and the river
all to here
    in the darkness
I love you
    the new found

99

one thing
    another
like voices
    thoughts
like maggots
     like ghosts or puns
beautifully various
      as scattered teeth
as blossom
    blackthorn winter
no one's ever prepared
      at the end of it
light opens up
     to make us small beneath
small creatures
     stumbling & shrinking
nothing we have done
     is adequate
there will be dawns
     more beautiful for our absence
but who
   will see them
see the sky
   god's glowing flesh

100

things are coins
        put 'em on your eyes, son!
at the end
        introduce a fresh scenario
don't just stop it
        rewind or scratch or whirl
the whole round loopy world
        that error
the set of rusted tramlines
        they ought to get around to taking up
but haven't
        these things are small coins
and the banknotes
        & the letters of credit?
don't think it through
        spend time at the harbour
it will be needed
        soon enough again
at this moment
        I need & love
you
   and this cold world
uncoined
        with things

Bishops Stortford, Autumn 2004–Spring 2005

www.ingramcontent.com/pod-product-compliance
Lightning Source LLC
Chambersburg PA
CBHW031157160426
43193CB00008B/406